WHO'S HOLIDAY!

A Comedy with a Twist of Rhyme

Matthew Lombardo

BROADWAY PLAY PUBLISHING INC
New York
www.broadwayplaypub.com
info@broadwayplaypub.com

Cover art by Fraver

First edition: April 2018
I S B N: 978-0-88145-758-2

Book design: Marie Donovan
Page make-up: Adobe InDesign
Typeface: Palatino

WHO'S HOLIDAY! was originally produced by
Whoville Theatrical, Scott and Jenny Beck, Jason Shaw,
Ken Fakler, Drew Desky/Dane Levens and Darren
Bagert at The Westside Theatre in New York City
opening on 20 November 2017. The cast and creative
contributors were:

CINDY LOU WHO..................................... Lesli Margherita

Director.. Carl Andress
Set design .... David Gallo
Lighting design .... Ken Billington & Jonathan Spencer
Costumes... Jess Goldstein
Sound design................................. Bart Fasbender
Wigs .... Charles LaPointe
Production stage manager .... Jeffry George

NOTE ON MUSIC

For performance of copyrighted songs, arrangements or recordings referenced in this play, permission of the copyright owner(s) must be obtained. See Music Rights page at the back of the book. Other songs, arrangements or recordings may be substituted provided permission from the copyright owner(s) of such songs, arrangements or recordings is obtained or songs, arrangements or recordings in the public domain may be substituted.

For Cindy Lou's rap song, producers should choose a backing track that reflects their vision of the production.

For Jordan Greenberger

CHARACTER & SETTING

CINDY LOU WHO, 45. *Unlike the bright-eyed character of her youth, she is no longer an innocent. Having been dealt a tough hand in the game of life, she desperately attempts to remain cheery in all situations. Despite her style-challenged attire and now poorly permed bleached blond hair, there still is a glimmer of hope in her beaten down spirit.*

A dilapidated trailer in the snowy hills of Mount Crumpit.

Time: Christmas Eve

WHO'S HOLIDAY! *is performed without an intermission.*

(The curtain rises on the interior of an older, modest, rundown trailer. The furniture is well worn, the carpet has cigarette burns, and the overall taste is reminiscent of 1970s suburbia. The home is decorated for the holiday, with colored lights strung around the windows, holly and cheap silver and gold garland, and a not so tasteful Christmas tree in the corner of the main room. There is one single stocking taped on the Kelvinator refrigerator. CINDY LOU WHO *enters from outside, holding a bag of ice. She puts the ice on the table, then takes off her coat and boots. As she slips into her high heels, she happens to glance out at the audience.)*

CINDY LOU WHO:
Oh hi! Well hello! I'm so glad that you're here.
But I can't talk that long cause it's that time of year.

See, I'm throwing a party tonight for some pals.
Just a little soiree for some guys and some gals.

I'd invite you to join, but my place is so small.
And if I let one, I'd have to let all.

But we can chat for a bit, until they all show.
And then I'm afraid—well—you'll all have to go.

(She puts her boots away, then edges closer to the audience.)

Oh, you all look so festive. Just bursting with cheer.
(Waving)
Hey mister! Hi lady! YASSS! QUEER IN THE REAR!

You remember me, right? Oh, I'm sure that you do.
When I was a youngster? I was Cindy Lou Who.

You recall my big eyes. My pink one piece pajama.
It was a present that year from my now dead great
  gramma.

Such an innocent I was. Oh, the ignorance of youth.
Then life starts to unfold and you get kicked in the
  tooth.

But I'm getting ahead. I don't mean to confuse.
I just hate Christmas Eve. As do some of you Jews.

See? My loathing stems from a deep-rooted place
In a town known as Who-ville, where I can't show my
  face.

You remember the city. So festive. So white.
Our holiday seasons were filled with delight.

How we'd sing "Fahoo Fores Dahoo Dores" with glee.
As we put goo-goo-gums and foo-foo-fluffs on the tree.

(Whatever the fuck those were.)

(She walks over to the kitchen table, placing the ice in a bucket.)

When you all saw me last, I was two, maybe three.
Twas the year I met Santa, or so he told me.

He wore the same clothing, the buckled suit and the
  hat.
But something had changed with this strange copycat.

He was green and quite large. Not man. Not beast.
He didn't look like Santa. No. Not in the least.

His real intent was to stop Christmas that year,
So he snuck into town with his doggy reindeer.

He came right into our home when we were all
  sleeping.
But then I heard a noise. So out of bed I went creeping.

I watched for awhile as he was stealin' our shit.
Then I cooed by mistake and he saw me. That twit.

"Why Santy Claus Why?" I asked him sincerely.
As he grunted and snorted and made his way near me.

He told me some lie about "electrical malfunction."
So fast with the fibs. So resourceful. Such gumption.

But I believed his whole story. That's what the young
  do.
I thought he was Santa—and his words were all true.

How would I know he was evil or crass?
He gave me some water. Then patted my ass.

(The telephone rings.)

Excuse me a moment. This needs my attention.
A guest might be lost and want some direction.

(She answers the phone. Into receiver:)

Hello. Merry Christmas. And how do you do?
Yup. You're speaking with me. Duh. It's Cindy Lou
  Who.

Oh hi Thidwick. *(To audience)* It's Thidwick, the big-
  hearted moose.
(Into phone) Where are you? What's happening? Come
over. Let loose.

(Disappointed) Oh. You can't? Oh no. I'm so sorry to
  hear.
An antler infection? It won't disappear?

No. That's okay. But it won't be the same.
Yes. Thank you for calling. *(She hangs up the phone.)*
  Ugh. That excuse was so lame.

All moose shed their antlers in winter, it's true.
I learned that from watching Captain Kangaroo.

But that's okay. Other friends will soon come.
And believe you me, they are fun, fun, fun, fun!

That silly moose can't upset me. I won't make a big
   stink.

I'll just get my party started with a holiday drink.

(She walks over to back of the trailer.)

Now let's see. I have Vodka. And bourbon. And gin on
   this table.

I'll just fix me a cocktail while y'all read your
   Playbill.

*(She picks up a bottle of gin in one hand and a bottle of vodka
in the other and pours them into the same mixing cup.)*

(They're both the same color so it's okay.)

*(She finishes making her drink and is just about to sip it
when she looks back out to the audience.)*

Oh. I'm sorry. You must think I'm so terribly rude.

Any drinkers out there? Anyone in the mood?

(She points to a gay man in the audience.)

You sir. Come up. Don't be shy. Don't be quiet.

Watch your step. There you go. Oh, I bet you're a riot!

(The MAN comes up onstage and she seats him at the table.)

CINDY LOU WHO:
What's your name?

MAN: _____

CINDY LOU WHO: Oh that's a nice tag.
From the way that you dress you look like a f- "Frank".

CINDY LOU WHO: Where you from?

MAN: _____

CINDY LOU WHO: _____? Oh. Well.
   That sounds majestic!
Me? I never left Whoville. Just a girl who's domestic.

(She gives an uncomfortable giggle and flirts.)

What do you do for a living? Something acclaimed?

MAN: _____

CINDY LOU WHO:
Oh. I see. Well. You should not be ashamed.

(Maybe a little ashamed.)

(She makes the two of them a drink.)

And now a quick splash of some nice, icy seltzer.
But not too much seltzer, so fasten your belt, sir!

(She sprays a squirt in each drink.)

You've got to handle the seltzer with care and with
  grace.
If you squeeze it too hard? It squirts right in your face.

(We all know someone like that, don't we?)

(She starts to hand him a drink, pulls back.)

You're not in A A or any of that nonsense?

MAN: _____.

CINDY LOU WHO: Cause I don't want your relapse on
  my fuckin' conscience.

(She hands him the drink.)

Here's to you, _____, my handsome sweet pup.
Merry Christmas. Happy Holidays. Okay. Bottoms up.

(They both take a sip. She spray spits it out.)

CINDY LOU WHO:
Whoa! This is strong. I have got to be careful.
One more of these and I'll sure be a handful.

*(She escalates the flirting, practically throwing herself on
him. After a moment, she realizes he is not responding. She
regains composure.)*

Well. It was nice meeting you, _____. You are a treat.
But clearly I'm the wrong gender. So go back to your
  seat.

(The MAN leaves.)

CINDY LOU WHO: (He wasn't as fun as I thought he'd
be.)

(She sees latecomers entering the theater.)

Oh look. They must have just opened the gate.
To let in the rude people who arrived here so late.

Oh no, don't mind us. We'll just wait. No. We're fine.
Let's just screw all the people who showed up here on
  time.

All settled now? You sure? We all set?
Don't get outta those seats. Oh and yeah, that's a
  threat.

(Under her breath:)

Ugh. These holiday tourists. They rev up my jets.
(To late comers)
God forbid you spend money and see the Rockettes.

What was I saying? Oh yes. That green freak.
Who took all our things and made our Christmas look
  bleak.

Well. The next morning came and we Whos were not
  happy.
With no toys to play with, the day was—well—crappy.

No jingtinglers. No pantookas. No skates for the
  meadow.
It's like we woke up and now lived in a ghetto.

(I'm sorry. Was that word offensive? It gets worse.)

Oh, I cried and I cried till I got a good slap.
My parents were not entertaining my crap.

They called me ungrateful, thankless and churlish.
They demanded I start acting more happy and girlish.

"Cindy", they said "Christmas ain't about gifts,
It's about joy and peace. Quit your cryin' and sniffs.

So the whole town got dressed and stood round the big
  tree
We sang that same song. Some folks were off key.

But we didn't let anyone spoil our tune
Cause we all had each other, in our Who-ville
  commune.

And that in itself was truly enough.
We Whos stood together in good times and tough.

And that love that we shared made me feel oh so swell
Though I still wanted a Malibu Barbie doll from Mattel.

(The doorbell rings.)

CINDY LOU WHO:
Ohh. My friends have arrived. I've now gotta go.
I'll catch up with you later. It was nice chatting, ya
know?

(The doorbell rings again.)

CINDY LOU WHO:
(Screaming) ONE MINUTE! I'M COMING! *(To herself)*
                                Oh, such holiday luck.
To be surrounded by friends.

*(She opens the door and a flurry of snowballs are thrown at
her.)*

                    JESUS CHRIST! WHAT THE FUCK??!

(We hear children's laughter as she screams out to them.)

CINDY LOU WHO:
YOU KIDS ARE IN TROUBLE. DON'T YOU READ?
  NO TRESPASSES!
YOU SHOW UP AGAIN AND I'LL KICK ALL YOUR
  ASSES!

*(She slams the door, grabs a towel and wipes the snow off her
face and dress. She turns back to the audience.)*

Well that wasn't nice. My spirits are dropping.
Just look at me now. My new dress is now sopping.
I need to go change. I'll be back in a twinkle.

(She moves behind a partition for a quick moment, instantly reappearing in a new dress.)

There. This is pretty. Not even a wrinkle.

(Just like *Dreamgirls*.)

Oh these kids now in Who-ville are so nasty and mean
But I'll get them back come next Halloween.

(I'm kidding. I would never put razor blades in apples. Again.)

I need to cheer myself up. I'll just take out my stash.
Have any of you ever smoked a pipe filled with Who
   Hash?

(She retrieves a bong and a baggie from behind the couch.)

Oh, don't you Ohhh and Ahhh me. It's like a
   prescription.
It keeps me in check. So don't have a conniption.

(She begins to stuff the hash in the bong pipe.)

You may not know this, but I suffer depression.
I don't do this a lot. Don't get that impression.

I've just had a tough life, which I'm sorting and dealing
And sometimes a smoke—well—it keeps me from
   feeling.

One quick puff then I'll see what my plan is.
Just give me a sec—

(She takes a large puff from the bong.)

                                   —oh, this shit is bananas.

Okay. So. Back to what happened on that one crazy
  Christmas.
As that Grinch rode away with our toys on the
  isthmus.

(Oh, I'm sorry. An "isthmus" is a little strip of land
forming a link between two larger parts of land,
usually joining structures, craters or clefts larger
than itself. I'm sure that went right over poor little
_____'s head. If he's dumb enough not to
rub his nose in between these babies he sure as fuck
doesn't know what an isthmus is. I'll just dumb things
down for you from now on. Okay princess?)

Well. All of a sudden, we hear this "boo-boo, boo-boo"
From a bugle high up on a hill out of view.

Then a sled tumbled down from that snowy white cliff
With that man-beast aboard, we remained rather stiff.

That creature, that ogre, who took everything.
Brought all our toys back when we started to sing.

And I thought to myself, how peculiar, how strange.
That someone like him was now able to change.

We Whos were so moved by his act of contrition
We invited him to share in our holiday tradition.

Christmas was a time to forgive and to care
We asked him to stay. We added a chair.

That Grinch sat to my left at our afternoon feast.
We even let him carve our delicious roast beast.

After dinner, he bravely told us the facts.
How he lived by himself with just his dog Max.

Such a sad little life, it brought a tear to my face
How he could live all alone in that faraway place.

Well. From that day forward, we became rather
  chummy
That green thing and I. He was charming. Funny!

He would drive into town in his little oxcart
He was thoughtful and kind—for an ugly old fart.

He taught me to skate, to ride my bike down the street.
He took me for ice cream. Ohhh. That monster was
    sweet.

Years flew by and we remained rather close.
My school chums didn't get it. They just thought he
    was gross.

But every so often you befriend someone offbeat.
Who can teach you new lessons. Make you complete.

I didn't care if he was different or not like the rest.
He treated me nicely. That's my only test.

I'm not going to fib, I can't even pretend.
That silly 'ol Grinch. He became my best friend.

But things started to change when I turned eighteen.
I was becoming a woman. And he? Was still green.

The night of my birthday, he took me alone to the
    dock.
Where he gave me my present. His big, thick, long—

(The telephone rings.)

(Excuse me.)

(She answers the telephone.)

Merry Christmas. Why aren't you here at my party?
Oh Yertle the Turtle. Yeah. I knew you'd be tardy.

What? I can't hear you? My phone's not connecting.
Oh. Congratulations my friend. Your wife is
    expecting?

How soon? How exciting! How thrilling! How nifty!
The doctor supposes she's due to have fifty?!

Oh. She's not feeling well. Yeah. Sure. No. I get it.
You're not stopping by? Don't worry. Don't sweat it.

Yes. And to you and your wife as well.
Merry Christmas. Happy New Year.
            (Screams) YOU CAN BOTH GO TO HELL!

(She slams down the receiver. Then:)

No turtles lay eggs in the winter. What a laugh!
I should grab my pernach and split his shell right in
half!

(Oh, I'm sorry. A "pernach" is a type of flanged mace
originating in the 12th century primarily used by
Russians in the region of Kiev. The pernach became
popular because it was capable of penetrating plate
armor, or the soldier's protective shells which is why
I thought it would be the perfect weapon to use on
Yertle because as a tortoise he also has a shell. Oh, just
look at poor little _____ who hasn't a clue as to what
I'm talking about up here. *(Calls to him)* You're gonna
have to Wikipedia all this shit when you get home.
Learning is fun, _____! *(Sings)* The more you
know!)

Well. Half of my guests are clearly not coming.
Calling this late. Their behavior is numbing.

But the others will be here. I know that they will.
They're just not that punctual. Where the hell's my
  Advil?

(She starts looking around the trailer.)

Oh fuck ibuprofen! I need something stronger.
I'm so nervous and edgy. I can't take this much longer.

*(She gets down on her hands and knees and looks under the
couch.)*

I know I dropped it somewhere. Oh poo. Damn it all.
Where is it? Wait. Found it. My last Tramadol!

*(She gets up from the floor with the pill in between her
fingers.)*

Can I take this with liquor? No? Yes? Maybe so?
Screw it. It's my party. Let me give it a go.

(She pops the pill and drinks the rest of the cocktail.)

There. Good. Yes. Great. I feel better already.
Although that cocktail has me feeling somewhat
  unsteady.

Please don't judge all my drinkin' n druggin'.
It's not like I'm out all night tweakin' n clubbin'.

(Anymore)

I'm really a homebody and just stay in this shelter.
And the liquor and pills—well—Mama needs a 'lil
  helper.

(She lights a cigarette.)

Where were we? Oh. Right. The first time I got laid.
And if you think black men are hung? Honey, try goin'
  jade.

When he first took it out, I almost ran 'way.
Cause that thing 'tween his legs grew three sizes that
  day!

But he was gentle and slow. He took his time with me
  then.
And once I relaxed? HE HIT IT AGAIN AND AGAIN!

Ohh, I was transported, oh yes, from my back to my
  front.
I 'specially liked when he'd stick his tongue in my—
  left ear.

(Beat)

(Ohhh, there are some dirty birds in this crowd. Dirty
birds! You all thought I was going to say "cunt".)

(She puts out the cigarette.)

Such new and strong feelings I had never felt before.
My heart was exploding for my sweet paramour.

I would meet every day with my secret new playmate
Then a month had gone by and I failed to menstruate.

(I know, right?)

Oh, I had to do something and do something quick.
I was nauseous and tired and in mornings so sick.

I went to the doctor who had me pee in a cup.
The test results confirmed: this bitch was knocked up.

I ran to the Grinch to relay my new finding
He just smiled and laughed. Found my news so
    exciting.

Then he kneeled before me, got down on one knee.
He took my hand in his claw and said: "Marry me".

My parents, however, weren't pleased in the least.
I mean, who wants their baby girl deflowered by a
    beast.

My mother was crying as Dad looked up from his
    desk.
A mixed marriage of color to them was grotesque.

I pleaded with them. "You don't understand!
I love him. I know it's not what you planned!"

My father, he grabbed me, locked me into my room.
"You'll stay up there, Missy! He will not be your
    groom!"

Hours and days passed as I started to plot.
Cause despite their displeasure—I was not throwin'
    away my—shot!

*(She grabs a microphone out of the stocking. The lights
change. Music)*

My name is Cindy Lou Who and I am here to say
If you have a shot in life don't go throw it away

Whether work or play or even crazy romance
Get out in the world—go take a chance

Now my mom and dad thought I was losing my mind
cause my achin' for that monster proved that love is
  blind
They couldn't understand, they looked at me with such
  awe
Cause they really didn't want to have a green son-in-
  law

Green son-in-law
Green son-in-law
They really didn't wanna have a green son-in-law

Now that grinch, he was ugly and yeah he was bad
But I became a plushie junkie and thought he was rad

His teeth were brown. He smelled kinda funky
But when we did the nasty I was his crazy monkey

Only eighteen—didn't know many mens
Now i'm lookin' in da phone book for o-b-g-y-n's

I had to be that grinch's wife, that was my goal
There was no way I'z birthin' without that 'ol troll
Without that 'ol troll
Without that 'ol troll
No way I'z be birthin' without that 'ol troll

Na na na
Na na na na
Na na na
Na na na na

Ev'ry touch, ev'ry move, ev'ry time that we kissed
I knew there and then I could no longer resist

So I planned to run 'way without any fuss
But my 'rents 'r all up in my shit, refuse to discuss

Their little Cindy Lou, who they spent years just lovin'
Now they're freakin cause I got this bun in the oven

I mean, what's the big deal? Why they shamin' on me?
It's not like I told them I came down with Hep C

Not gettin' Hep C
Not gettin' Hep C
Cindy Lou was never gonna get herself no Hep C
I never, never, never thought that I would go green
when I was just a girl, it never did seem

It was what I really wanted but my heart 'n my mind
Was pried open at last so I can finally find

A life full of love, without bigotry
Why can't we just let people be who they be

Without discrimination or narrow-mindedness, see?
Just love who you want. don't you agree?

(The lights change back. Music ends.)

Betcha didn't see that comin' or expect that to hap
Despite what you think, some white girls can rap.

(She places the microphone back into the stocking.)

So anyway.

(She is breathing heavy.)

So anyway.

(Breathing more)

Hold on. I'm all out of breath.

(She takes another cigarette, lights it, inhales.)

Much better.

So anyway. I starved myself in my room without
    friends
Until the fourth day my parents came to make their
    amends

They opened my door. They said they were sorry.
They brought be some cheese and some fresh calamari.

Dad said he'd forgive my little moral evasion
If I promised to marry a boy who at least was
    Caucasian.

From that weird Scottish clan, he brought in Morris
    McGurk,
the kid from next door who I thought was a jerk.

Morris, now a young man, seemed rather nervous.
He got Dad's approval cause he just bought a circus.

(Who the fuck buys a circus?)

But if I pledged to marry Morris, my parents would
    forgive
and release my large dowry on which we could live.

(The oven timer buzzes.)

Oh. Wait. Stop. Hold on to your nerves.
I don't want to burn my tasty hors d'oeuvres.

*(She places oven mitts on her hand, walks over to the kitchen
and takes out a tray from the oven.)*

Oh, these came out so well. So warm and nutritious.
Anyone want to taste? I swear they're delicious.

Oh. So many are hungry out there, don't you know.
You freaks should really eat before you come to a
    show.

*(She walks down into the audience and offers hors
d'oeuvres.)*

There you go. One each please. Let me serve. Please
    don't yank it.

(To an older woman)

Do you know what these are?

OLDER WOMAN: Pigs in a blanket?

CINDY LOU WHO: Yes. Pigs in a blanket!

(We have a smart one on this side. Unlike poor
_____ over there who was too stupid to make a
move on me. "Oh, I'm afraid of boobies. What do I do
with them? Play Toss Across?")

(To the woman)

What's you name, sweetie?

OLDER WOMAN: _____

CINDY LOU WHO:
Oh, _____. Nice to meet you, honey.
And that ring on your finger! You must come from
  money.

How 'bout you people back there? You all want some
  treats?

*(She pretends to walk back then quickly turns toward the
stage.)*

Tough shit. Next time buy better seats.

(Cheap T K T S bastards.)

(She responds to their reaction.)

CINDY LOU WHO: Oh really? You want to start
  something, Mister Man with the Cup?
Don't make me come back there, bitch I'll fuck you
  right up.

(She throws an hors d'oeuvre at him.)

Aren't these just yummy? They were made with good
  fats.
But I couldn't afford meat so I made them with rats.

(Oh, I'm just kidding. *(Under her breath)* No. I'm not)

Okay. That's enough. You don't need to be pests.
Let's get back to my story and leave some for my
  guests.

(She gets back onstage.)

So. I agreed to marry Morris and swore I'd not falter.
But on the day of my wedding, I left McGurk at the
  altar.

I ran away from Who-Ville into the arms of the Grinch.
I never looked back. Not once did I flinch.

We were married days later despite all the objection.
And so we were wed 'mongst a small weird collection.

Horton was there and the Cat in the Hat.
The Lorax showed up. And oh gurrrl, she got fat.

The Sneetches and Wocket brought that obstinate Sam
Who is now totally vegan. So no green eggs and ham.

(Why did we go through all that for?)

Our wedding was lovely on top of Mount Crumpit.
We exchanged our vows there. Thing Two played the
    trumpet.

My wedding gown was stunning, a sight to be seen
We were married by Sylvester McMonkey McBean.

Such a special occasion but all the Whos stayed away.
My parents and friends, they disowned me that day.

Some folks don't accept couples that are diverse.
Some people think certain loves are perverse.

But I didn't care what anyone said.
I followed my heart. And so I was wed.

After the reception I moved right into his cave
But it wasn't a cave. It looked more like a grave!

It was dreary and dark and smelled like you'd think.
No toilet. No plumbing. No kitchen. No sink.

How could anyone actually live in this hell?
In Who-ville everything was so bright and pastel.

I had to make the most of this new situation
So I gave it a makeover to reduce my frustration.

I rolled up my sleeves, and oh, I cleaned each
little nook, every corner with bleach, bleach, bleach,
    bleach.

I went down to Who Depot and purchased a drape,
some towels and rugs, to change the landscape.

I hung pictures and prints and several dried flowers
Oh the time that I spent. That remodel took hours.

But soon with my touch, we now had a nice place.
I looked at my husband. He had a smile on his face.

Oh, I loved that green manbeast. I swear that I did.
And soon it came time for me to pop out that kid.

Ohh. My labor was tough. My contractions were
    numerous.
And I freaked when I saw what came outta my uterus.

See, my child was not a small bundle of joy
But a large glob of green. Was it a girl or a boy?

With the fur and the paws it looked just like its Daddy.
With no who dilly attached, I named the girl Patti.

So we started a family, as I lay there beside her
I hoped my husband would be a decent provider.

But I soon realized he hadn't a job.
He just sat around all day being a great, big, fat slob.

So I tried to get work—filled out application,
    application.
But no Who would hire me after I made such a
    sensation.

They all knew I ran off with that 'ol scary monster
So no one would help us or offer to sponsor

A meal or clothing or any knitwear.
We even got denied for WhoShield health care.

(This was before Obama.)

Life was tough. We were poor and on the downswing.
And my husband turned right back into a nasty old
    thing.

He didn't help me find food or care about clothing.
That Grinch just sat on his ass—increasing my
  loathing.

What a fool I was. I should have married McGurk.
That was it. I called Morris and I begged him for work.

He took pity on me, brought me right into the loop
I worked at his circus and cleaned elephant poop.

The next few years we scraped by on my income
I didn't make much money. But at least it was some.

But it all soon went south when the folks from PETA
  came to town.
They took away all the animals. Shut that circus right
  down.

I asked Morris, "How? —How could they do this to
  you?"
But before he could answer, they took Morris away too.

I later found out what had caused all that drama.
Morris was having relations. With a twelve year old.
  Llama!

It went from bad to worse by that next Christmas
  Evenin'
Patti was now seven. We were hungry and freezin'.

I went outside for a smoke and to ponder my woes
When I saw our dog Max had turned icy and froze.

My dumb spouse forgot to bring him in the night prior.
I rushed Max inside. Put him next to the fire.

But despite my attempt, there was no winning path.
Max was dead.
                    We were starving.
                              That's right. Do the math.

I put Max in the oven now I know this might sicken-
But I sliced him and served. Dog tastes just like
  chicken.

(A paper airplane flies through the open window and lands on the couch.)

Oh, would you look at this here. This small paper jet.
I know what this is. It's another regret.

Well. Let's read it and see what this letter produces
and who now is cancelling and what their excuse is.

(She opens the paper, reads:)

"Dear Cindy Lou. I know this is sudden and awfully
  rash
but we sadly can no longer come to your holiday bash.

We had every intention to show up at your trailer
but my wife had an asthma attack and lost her inhaler.

The four of us all send you a holiday kiss,
Signed, One, Two, Red and Blue Fish".

(Beat)

FISH HAVE GILLS!! HOW CAN THEY HAVE
ASTHMA ATTACKS??!!

(Then:)

Oh, I know what is happening. They won't say it to my
  face.
But no one is brave enough to show up at my place.

See the last part of my story is where it gets twisted.
And you soon will all learn how I got—well—black
  listed.

So I already told you how I cooked up our hound
But the end of my tale I'm sure will astound.

See? When my husband dug in he started to holler.
As he was chewing his food he bit into the collar.

"It's your fault!" I screamed, irate and upset.
"You don't have a job! So we're eating our pet!"

Enraged, he came at me cursing and swinging.
I ran out of the cave—as I heard the bells ringing.

Christmas Day had arrived. The sun was just peeking.
The Whos began waking. Their front doors all
   creaking.

I saw my family and friends gather 'round that same
   tree.
How I loved that tradition, when I was just three.

Then my husband came out with a rock in his mitt.
It was him or me now. I don't put up with that shit.

He lunged for me, soon moving in for the kill.
I stepped quick to the left and he slipped down the hill.

Thousands of feet my husband would fall.
The saddest part was? I wasn't that sad at all.

The police soon arrived when they found his dead
   carcass
I didn't shed a tear. They all thought I was heartless.

They dragged me downtown and began all their
   questions
I couldn't afford counsel so I relied on suggestions.

They charged me that night with a murder offense.
I pleaded with them. "It was just self defense!"

It was in all the papers and on T V shows.
All the whispers and gossip people chose to suppose.

They called me a killer. Some cold hearted wife.
Who had plotted and planned to take her own
   husband's life.

But I didn't do anything 'cept protect myself and my
   child.
But the press had a field day. The rumors grew wild.

No one believed sweet Cindy Lou Who.
They just painted me as some sick, psychopath shrew.

I watched those twelve people the lawyers did choose
a jury of my peers, all consisting of Whos.

They found me guilty. And said that I lied.
They charged me with murder and with yes,
  "canicide".

They put me in handcuffs for all of my slaughter.
I watched as they soon took away my young daughter.

They first took my kid to my parents for protection
But when they saw what she looked like, she got their
  rejection.

They didn't want other Who families to know of this
  grandchild
So they slammed their front door, and Patti was exiled.

She was placed soon enough in an orphanage cage
Where she would stay until she was of legal age.

The last time I saw Patti was in that one courtroom
  pew
My last words to her were, "Mommy loves you".

Two guards threw me in a van like some Who-Villy
  trash
As the paparazzi took pictures, all the cameras did
  flash

We went for a long ride, till we arrived in fresh hell
At a prison located in Motta-fa-Potta-fa-Pell

*(The lights immediately change to a harsher look as we hear a
metal door slam. Cue underlying music)*

They led me through the front gate past the mirrored
  reflector
Where I first had to step through a metal detector.

They ripped my clothes off, a time of such gravity
While a female matron began searching my cavity

(And I ain't talkin' dental.)

I was placed in a holding cell. All the inmates abuzz.
Then I was interviewed by some bitch who looked like
  Gertrude McFuzz.

The reality of my plight began to soon hit
As they determined which building would be my unit.

For twelve long months I sat alone in my cell
I had no comb. No barrettes. Not even hair gel.

All my past choices now seemed oh so wrong.
I got involved with a Grinch—which was wrong all
   along.

It was Christmas Eve once again, but so much had
   changed.
No singing. No smiling. No gifts were exchanged.

I so wanted to be young once again and not grown.
But I was no longer a girl. I had a girl of my own.

I could feel my heart breaking. My spirit was slain.

(Cue music)

CINDY LOU WHO: To take a child from her mother?
   There is no greater pain.

*(Suggested song: "Blue Christmas" or another ballad that
invokes the feel of being separated from a loved one)*

CINDY LOU WHO: *(Spoken, building)*
I should have never left my family. I brought them
   such disgrace.
And what I thought was real love turned out to be
   misplaced.

I gave up everything to be with him, my childhood,
   and my home.
And what did that get me?! Huh? Cause I am stuck
   here all alone.

(Sings final verse. The song ends as the lights resume.)

CINDY LOU WHO: (So, that was the downer part of
the show. Oh yeah, we drop the penny deep here in
_____.)

A few days later, I was transferred to a cell that was
  permanent
As I passed by some female felons having a bridge
  tournament.

But the cell where they put me was smaller than the
  first.
Two bunk beds and a toilet. Oh yeah. It got worse.

So I laid on the bottom bed and tried to get rest
But I soon was awakened by a ferocious new guest.

This bossy old woman who was loud and was large
She was my new cellmate who they called Bad-Mouth
  Marge.

"Whatcha doin' on my bed?! The bottom bunk Marge
  owns!
Get your ass off that mattress, you sad bag 'o bones!"

"I'm so sorry" I trembled. I was scared and was
  shaken.
"Yeah, well don't do it again or I'll fry your damn
  bacon!"

(I had no idea what she was talking about but it didn't
sound like something I would particularly enjoy).

"Whatcha in for, Petunia? Tell Marge whatcha did.
Did ya write some bad checks? Did ya diddle some
  kid?"

"They think I killed my husband, that's what they say
  I've done.
But I swear I didn't do it. That's my 4-1-1."

"We all didn't do it." Marge approved in her spewin'.
"I killed my mans too cause my sister he was screwin'.

So I shot her first, then cut him up with a knife
It's no one's surprise that I'm in here for life".

Okay. Now I was horrified. I did not like Marge fully.
I mean, I did not want to live with another mean bully.

"One more thing and we'll get along fine".
"What is it?" I asked. "STOP TALKING IN RHYME!"
"But that's how all the Whos talk" I tried to explain.
"Well you ain't no Who here! It's time you speak
    plain!"
"Don't tell me what to do!" I unexpectedly blared.
As Marge came toward me with her nostrils all flared.
"Don't make me hurt you!" as Marge moved into my
    space.
I didn't know how to respond—so I spit in her face.

Well that was it. I just thought I was dead.
But what Marge did next was so surprising instead.

She reached out her hand and said "Good for you.
Ya need to be tough and a little cuckoo

To survive in this place!" Marge bellowed with pride.
And as I shook her soft hand, I started to cry.

Marge sat me down, put her arm 'round my shoulder.
"Listen to someone who's a little wiser and older".

She wiped 'way my tears, rubbed the hair on my head
And she started to rock me as she turned and she said.

"Listen up, Buttercup. Lockup is hell.
Don't let on that you're scared if you wanna excel".

I knew she was right. I'd have to fight daily wars
If I was gonna survive with these skanks and these
    whores".

Marge taught me how to make the most of my difficult
    plight.
I worked in the laundry. Made crafts at night.

Together with Marge it all became bearable
My life wasn't over. It was completely repairable.

I started taking college courses online every week.
Biology. Alegbra. I even learned me some Greek.

After years of hard study, I got an online degree
I majored in business through DeVry University.

(It's accredited)

I was no longer puzzled, perturbed or perplexed.
I even tried me some of that lesbian sex.

(It wasn't half bad. *(Points to woman)* You know what
I'm talking about. *(...)* Yeah you do. *(...)* You totally do.)

Ten years into my sentence I had brains. I had brawn.
But one summer morning I saw that Marge was now
    gone.

"Where is she?!" I screamed. "What'd ya do with my
    pal?!"
Marge had been transferred to another jail by the canal.

I slept in her bed in that now quiet cell
I could still feel her there. I could still smell her smell.

I missed that old coot. Oh, I missed Marge a lot.
But soon this new bitch was sitting on her old cot.

"Get off that bed, Missy!" I screamed at that girl.
"I sleep there now!" Ooo, she got my skirts in a twirl!

This scared, little thing, she just started to weep
I didn't mean to upset her. I'm not some, mean creep.

My heart went out to this lost little tyke.
I was in her shoes once. I know what that's like.

So I gave her the same talk that 'ol Marge she gave me.
With an arm on her shoulder and a hand on her knee.

A few years later, I was jumping with glee
I had made my parole. They were setting me free.

I said goodbye to the girls, I was no longer broken.
I gathered my things as the jail door slid open.

*(The lights immediately change back as we hear a metal door
slam. The underlying music stops.)*

CINDY LOU WHO:
Ya know, in prison I stumbled upon what I needed to
    find.
It was me that I found, all that time being confined.

Cause you wanna know somethin'? And this is the
    truth.
Cindy Lou Who is not the girl of her youth.

There's a force out there so loving and giving.
Whatever that is takes care of all that is living.

So I guess I am grateful for all that's transpired.
It made me stronger and wiser. It's what was required.

Sometimes in life, good people do some bad stuff.
But they can get back on track if they want to enough.

So surround yourself with people that are kind and
    who care.
If they don't treat you that way, then watch out.
    Beware.

And as far as romance goes? Ha. I don't have advice.
Love is crazy. Love is awful. Love is—well—sometimes
    it's nice.

Just be leery of the ones who won't budge one damn
    inch.
Cause listen up ladies and gays: a Grinch stays a
    Grinch.

They released me last month for my good behavior
My great uncle who died—he, umm, left me this
    trailer.

As for my Patti, I've never seen her again.
She has her own life with her new family and friends.

How many times did I try to reach out?
But she blames me I guess. Has such anger. Such
    doubt.

She's a young woman now and looks like my clone
Well, that is, if you overlook her greenish skin tone.

Rumor has it she's happy, so gifted, such smarts,
She actually chose a career in the performing arts.

After studying voice with coach Maurice DeCricked
She now plays Elphaba in the National Tour of *Wicked*.

(She's talented.)

Spending Christmas with Patti would have been so
   ideal
Well maybe next year when her emotions can heal.

That's why I threw this party, to make things more
   easy
Cause Christmas Eves always make me so anxious
   and—

(The telephone rings. Softly to herself:)

            —queasy.

*(The telephone rings again. She stares at it for a moment.
Sadly, she picks up the receiver. Into phone:)*

CINDY LOU WHO:
You don't have to tell me. I know you're not comin'.
Oh stop with the lies! Cant you just be forthcomin'?

None of you want to be seen with me now?
Because of my past? You all disavow.

Well. I thank you for calling. And speaking with
   reason.
Yes. And to you all as well. You enjoy the bright
   season.

(She hangs up the phone. Pause)

Well. I'm afraid that is that. No one will be showing.
I might as well turn off the lights.

(She gets up and turns off a few lamps.)

                        Oh look. It's snowing.

(She looks out the window for a moment.)

So many people are out there tonight.
In the arms of their loved ones. Holding them tight.

Tomorrow they'll wake and exchange a nice gift.
Having someone here now would give my spirit a lift.

(She takes the blanket off the back of couch.)

Ehh. It's just another day. It will all be over soon.
I should go to bed now. Sleep way past noon.

(She lays down on the couch and covers herself with the blanket.)

I tried to reach out to all of my friends.
But they don't want to be friends. So this is how it all
 ends.

You should go home now to the people you love.
I'll be fine. I'm okay. Well. Maybe. Kind of.

(She quietly begins crying on the couch. Long pause)

Why are you still sitting there looking at me?
Don't you have places that you need to be?

You don't have to stay. I don't want your damn pity.
There are so many things to do and see in the city.

(Pause)

And yet you remain. None of you stir.
Maybe I was wrong about who my friends really were.

All of this time you've been in front of my eyes.
We laughed and we talked. I had fun with you guys.

I have an idea. Now just lend me your ear.
But would you like to spend Christmas Eve with me
 here?

(The audience responds.)

CINDY LOU WHO:
_____? Would you? And _____would

you stay too?
We'll have our own party. We all will make do.

Hey. I know. Let's all sing a song by the pine!
You all can do harmony. But the melody's mine.

Ohh. But I don't have a piano cause I just have this one
  room.
Wait. I know how we'll be able to carry a tune.

I will open this box. A rare musical thing.

(She opens a nearby music box. It begins to play.)

Oh, that's just perfect. Come on friends. Let's sing.

(Suggested song: "Have Yourself a Merry Little Christmas"
or another heartwarming holiday carol)

CINDY LOU WHO: *(Interjections during song)*

(Okay, now shut the fuck up cause this part is just me)

(You see where Patti got it from, right?)

(Everyone! Even you people in the cheap seats!)

(Some of you should have taken the octave lower)

(At end of song, she speaks:)

It's been so wonderful spending time with you folks.
You were such a great crowd. You got most of the
  jokes.

But before you all go, I just want to say this
And I hope it brings all of you some seasonal bliss.

(Sings)

I wish you a Merry Christmas
I wish you a Merry Christmas
I wish you a Merry Christmas
And a Happy New Year

(The doorbell rings.)

Ugh. I'm sure it's those kids from before who were
  bratty.

(She walks to the front window, peeks out.)

Wait. That's not them. Oh my God!

(She turns to the audience. Screams)

IT'S PATTI!!!

(Blackout)

END OF PLAY

MUSIC RIGHTS

For permission to use the song *Blue Christmas* in performances, contact:

> Universal Music Publishing
> and The Judy J Olmsted Trust
> www.umusicpub.com

For permission to use the song *Have Yourself a Merry Little Christmas* in performances, contact:

> Sony/ATV Music Publishing
> Director of Theatrical Development
> www.sonyatv.com

www.ingramcontent.com/pod-product-compliance
Lightning Source LLC
Chambersburg PA
CBHW070036110426
42741CB00035B/2796